Snoopy

My Greatest Adventures

SPARKLER BOOKS

AN IMPRINT OF PHAROS BOOKS • A SCRIPPS HOWARD COMPANY

NEW YORK

Originally published and produced by
Arnoldo Mondadori Editore S.p.A., Milano

LC 88-042736 11524
ISBN 0-88687-377-0

Printed in Italy

Sparkler Books
An Imprint of Pharos Books
A Scripps Howard Company
200 Park Avenue
New York, NY 10166

10   9   8   7   6   5   4   3   2   1

CONTENTS

9   INTRODUCTION

10   PRESENTING... SNOOPY

14   JOE COOL

16   THE RED BARON

20   SNOOPY THE WRITER

23   SNOOPY AND SPORTS

28   SNOOPY AND SPIKE

29   SNOOPY AND WOODSTOCK

34   SNOOPY AND CHARLIE BROWN

37   SNOOPY AND LUCY

40   SNOOPY AND LINUS

43   SNOOPY AND THE REST OF THE WORLD

Snoopy was born at the Daisy Hill Puppy Farm. His father's occupation was probably much like that of other beagles. He chased his quota of rabbits and retired early. Snoopy's memories of the Daisy Hill Puppy Farm seem to be mostly good ones. We are told that he especially used to enjoy the beautiful summer evenings.

Lately, Snoopy's career as a World War I flying ace has been replaced with that of a barnstormer. He is also well into a career as a novelist. Once, he almost gained immortality as a baseball player when he had the opportunity to become the first player to tie Babe Ruth's homerun record. Unfortunately, Snoopy was beaten out by Hank Aaron.

There are many dreams left, and dreams of the future are just as good as dreams of the past. Lying on top of a dog house enables one, also, to look upward. This is the advantage that he has over the rest of us. What a lucky dog.

Presenting... Snoopy

IT'S ALMOST TIME...

SIGH

I'D BETTER GET DRESSED..

WHEN YOU APPEAR BEFORE THE HEAD BEAGLE, YOU ALWAYS WEAR BLACK...

I'D LOOK GREAT WITH SIDEBURNS!

© 1968 United Feature Syndicate, Inc.

WELCOME TO "NATURE TIME"

FISH EAT THE INSECTS, BIRDS EAT THE FISH, CATS EAT THE BIRDS...

THAT'S ENOUGH!

I DON'T WANT TO KNOW ABOUT IT

I HEAR THE FLAPPING OF WINGS...

LOOK AT THAT STUPID BIRD, WILL YOU?

HE THINKS HE'S GOING TO BUILD A NEST ON TOP OF MY STOMACH...

THE NERVE OF HIM! THE UNMITIGATED GALL! HIM AND HIS TWIGS AND STRING...

BY GOLLY, I'M GOING TO FIX HIS WAGON!

THE NEXT TIME HE COMES, I'M GOING TO GIVE HIM SUCH A TUSSLE, HE WON'T KNOW WHAT HIT HIM! I'LL TWIST HIS BEAK AND TIE KNOTS IN HIS TAIL...I'LL STIR HIS FEATHERS!

I CAN'T STAND IT!

GET READY, BIRD! THIS IS IT!

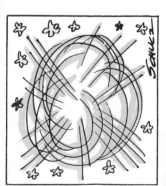

Joe Cool

NO ONE EVER INVITES JOE COOL HOME FOR THANKSGIVING...

HERE'S JOE COOL HANGING AROUND THE CAMPUS ON THANKSGIVING DAY..

EVERYTHING IS CLOSED... EVERYONE HAS GONE HOME... NO CHICKS... NOTHING !

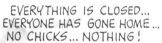

NO ONE INVITED JOE COOL HOME FOR THANKSGIVING SO HE'S BUYING A HAMBURGER AND A MALT AT A DRIVE-IN...

BLEAH!

HERE'S JOE COOL HANGING AROUND THE BEACH DRINKING ROOT BEER AND EYEING CHICKS

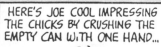

HERE'S JOE COOL IMPRESSING THE CHICKS BY CRUSHING THE EMPTY CAN WITH ONE HAND...

STUPID CAN !

14

The Red Baron

IT'S A LONG WAY TO..

TIPPERARY 1 Block →

☼ SIGH ☼

HERE'S THE WORLD WAR I FLYING ACE ZOOMING THROUGH THE AIR IN HIS SOPWITH CAMEL..

SUDDENLY HE SEES A SHADOW MOVE ACROSS THE GROUND..AN ANGRY SOUND FILLS THE AIR!

IT'S THE RED BARON! HE'S RIDDLING MY PLANE WITH BULLETS

THIS COULD RUIN MY WHOLE CHRISTMAS!

PRISON! THEY THREW ME IN PRISON!

WHY DID I HAVE TO GIVE MYSELF AWAY IN THAT RESTAURANT? WHY DID I GO OVER AND TALK TO THE RED BARON?

NOW, I'LL SPEND THE REST OF WORLD WAR I IN THIS PRISON...THEY'LL NEVER LET ME OUT! NEVER!

OWOOOOO

IT IS A COOL, CLEAR MORNING AS THE WORLD WAR I FLYING ACE WALKS ONTO THE FIELD... "GOOD MORNING, CHAPS"

CONTACT!

HERE'S THE WORLD WAR I FLYING ACE TAKING OFF IN HIS SOPWITH CAMEL

AS I PASS OVER THE FRONT LINES, I CAN SEE BURSTS OF ARTILLERY FIRE BELOW ME...

GREAT SCOTT! AN ENEMY OBSERVATION BALLOON!

THE WINGS ON MY PLANE SHRIEK IN PROTEST AS I TURN SHARPLY TO GET INTO POSITION...

GOOD GRIEF! MY GUNS ARE JAMMED!

I CAN'T LET THAT BALLOON GET AWAY...

AS MY PLANE DIVES PAST THE BALLOON, I LEAP OUT AT THE OBSERVER!

GRMF! OUCH! WAR! AUGH! POW! GROFGH! FIRE! BRFGH!

© 1967 United Feature Syndicate, Inc.

SOME OF THOSE BALLOON OBSERVERS ARE PRETTY TOUGH...

17

Snoopy the Writer

As he touched her hand, she sighed...

STOP RAINING ON MY NOVEL!

The

A GOOD WRITER WILL SOMETIMES SEARCH HOURS FOR JUST THE RIGHT WORD!

Dear Miss Manners,

Is it polite for a friend to sit on your nose?

Please excuse mY typpimg.

When he's Sitting th×re, i kant seee.

S.W.A.K.

Dear Sweetie, Have you missed me?

I think about you all the time. I can hardly wait until Sunday morning. Don't forget.

I THINK I'M IN LOVE!

RATS!

IT'S HOPELESS!

IF I'M GOING TO WORK AT NIGHT, I'M GOING TO HAVE TO HAVE AN INDOOR STUDIO...

YOU CAN'T WRITE BY FIREFLY!!

21

Snoopy and Sports

OLGA KORBUT HAS BEEN BUGGING ME FOR LESSONS!

HERE'S THE WORLD FAMOUS SURGEON OUT FOR HIS MORNING JOG...

IT'S RAINING AND THE WIND IS BLOWING..

WHAT AM I DOING OUT HERE?

I COULD BE IN A NICE WARM OPERATING ROOM!

HERE'S THE WORLD FAMOUS FOOTBALL COACH WALKING OUT ONTO THE FIELD

WINNING IS EVERYTHING! LOSING IS LIKE NOTHING!

THIS YEAR WE'RE GOING TO STRESS PHYSICAL CONDITIONING.. LOTS OF PUSH-UPS AND PLENTY OF RUNNING...

WOODSTOCK ALWAYS HAS TROUBLE WITH PUSH-UPS

STRIKE THREE!

DON'T WORRY, SNOOPY, YOU'LL GET TO BAT AT LEAST TWO MORE TIMES...

BY THE WAY, TEETH MARKS ARE NOT GOOD FOR YOUR BAT...

THIS IS IT...IF WE GET THIS LAST GUY, WE WIN...IF HE HITS ONE, WE LOSE...

IT'S A HIGH FLY BALL TO SNOOPY....IF HE CATCHES IT, WE WIN!!

NO PROBLEM

HEY! WHO'S THE SHORTSTOP WITH THE BIG NOSE?

BIG NOSE?!!

BONK!

WELL, WE LOST OUR FIRST GAME OF THE SEASON...

I WONDER HOW OUR NEW MANAGER WILL TAKE THIS DEFEAT?

BOOT! BOOT! BOOT!

BOOT! BOOT! BOOT!

I HATE LOSING!

Snoopy and Spike

Snoopy and Woodstock

POOR WOODSTOCK

HE'LL NEVER KNOW THE JOY OF WAKING UP ON CHRISTMAS MORNING, AND FINDING A NEW BICYCLE PARKED UNDER THE CHRISTMAS TREE...

I'D BETTER GO OVER, AND CONSOLE HIM...

? SIGH

I HATE PLAYING "BAT"!

I HATE IT WHEN HE PLAYS "ELEVATOR"!

29

8903968

Snoopy and Charlie Brown

BUT YOU DON'T HAVE ANY IDEA WHERE SHE IS!

HOW WILL YOU FIND HER? WHERE WILL YOU LOOK? DON'T YOU THINK YOU SHOULD CONSIDER THIS A LITTLE MORE CAREFULLY BEFORE YOU JUST SORT OF TAKE OFF?

NO, YOUR MIND IS MADE UP, ISN'T IT? WELL, I HATE TO SEE YOU GO, BUT GOOD LUCK, OL' PAL... I HOPE YOU FIND HER...

MOM!

YOU WERE ONLY TWO BLOCKS FROM HOME..

TWO BLOCKS? WE WERE GONE FOR A WEEK, AND WE ONLY GOT TWO BLOCKS FROM HOME?

SNOOPY!! WHAT ARE YOU DOING HERE?!

WHY WERE YOU TIED UP? WHAT HAPPENED TO YOU? I THOUGHT YOU HAD GONE SOUTH...

WELL, WE'LL HAVE TO LOOK AT IT THIS WAY... IF WE HAD FOUND OUR WAY SOUTH, WE PROBABLY WOULD HAVE MISSED THE HOCKEY SEASON..

WHAT ARE YOU DOING IN HERE?

DON'T TELL ME YOU'RE AFRAID OF THINGS THAT GO "BUMP" IN THE NIGHT?

I'M NOT AFRAID OF ANYTHING THAT GOES "BUMP" IN THE NIGHT. WHAT SHAKES ME UP ARE THOSE THINGS THAT GO..

AAUGH!

34

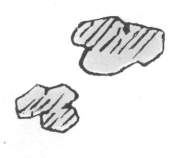

35

HERE.. YOU GOT A LETTER FROM MISS HELEN SWEETSTORY..

MISS HELEN SWEETSTORY, AUTHOR OF "THE SIX BUNNY-WUNNIES AND THEIR WATER BED"!! SHE ANSWERED MY FAN LETTER!

MISS HELEN SWEETSTORY TOUCHED THIS ENVELOPE WITH HER HANDS! THIS IS TOO MUCH!

OOOOOO! KLUNK!

HERE, YOU GOT AN OFFICIAL LETTER..

OOO! I LOVE OFFICIAL LETTERS!

AT LEAST YOU KNOW THAT IT'S NOT A TRAFFIC CITATION..

DOGS NEVER GET TRAFFIC CITATIONS NOR JURY DUTY

THAT'S WHAT IS KNOWN AS "SMALL CONSOLATION"!

AFGHAN PUPPIES FOR SALE..BOXERS, ONE HUNDRED DOLLARS AND UP...COLLIE PUPS FOR SALE...

"DOBERMAN PUPS...ENGLISH SETTER, REGISTERED, FIFTY DOLLARS... IRISH SETTERS, SEVENTY-FIVE DOLLARS, POODLES, SPRINGERS, CORGI PUPS..."

SMACK

I'M GLAD I ALREADY HAVE A HOME!

AND I GOT A VALENTINE FROM JOYCE AND I GOT ONE FROM PEGGY

AND I GOT ONE FROM ZELMA, AND JANELL, AND BOOTS AND PAT, AND SYDNEY, AND WINNIE, AND JEAN, AND ROSEMARY, AND COURTNEY, AND FERN, AND MEREDITH ...

AND AMY, AND JILL, AND BETTY, AND MARGE, AND KAY, AND FRIEDA, AND ANNABELLE, AND SUE, AND EVA, AND JUDY, AND RUTH ...

AND BARBARA, AND OL' HELEN, AND ANN, AND JANE, AND DOROTHY, AND MARGARET, AND...

I CAN'T STAND IT... I JUST CAN'T STAND IT...

Snoopy and Lucy

"CLOSE DANCING" IS COMING BACK!

I WOULDN'T VOTE FOR YOU IF YOU WERE THE LAST BEAGLE ON EARTH!

WAAH!

ALL RIGHT! IF YOU WERE THE LAST BEAGLE ON EARTH, I'D VOTE FOR YOU!

CAMPAIGN STRATEGY!

CLOMP!

Snoopy and Linus

I'M NOT GOING TO WRITE TO THE GREAT PUMPKIN THIS YEAR, SNOOPY..

INSTEAD, I'M GOING TO WRITE A LETTER TO THE HEAD BEAGLE... HOW DOES THAT STRIKE YOU?

FORGET IT!

© 1969 United Feature Syndicate, Inc.

THE HEAD BEAGLE HATES JUNK MAIL!

HERE'S THE WORLD FAMOUS ATTORNEY ON HIS WAY TO THE COURTHOUSE...

THIS IS A MAXIM OF JURISPRUDENCE..."A THING CONTINUES TO EXIST AS LONG AS IS USUAL WITH THINGS OF THIS NATURE"

DID YOU UNDERSTAND THAT?

I DIDN'T EVEN UNDERSTAND THE LUNCH MENU!

© 1985 United Feature Syndicate, Inc.

HERE...I FOUND THESE, AND THOUGHT YOU MIGHT LIKE TO HAVE THEM..

HOW NICE..

© 1971 United Feature Syndicate, Inc.

IF 3-D COMES BACK, I'M READY!

41

Snoopy and the Rest of the World